BARBARA L. PEACOCK

♦♦♦

SOUL CARE

in

AFRICAN AMERICAN PRACTICE

WORKBOOK

Urban Ministries, Inc.

Published in the United States by Urban Ministries, Inc.
P. O. Box 436987
Chicago, IL 60643
urbanministries.com 1-800-860-8642

ISBN 978-1-68353-726-7 (print)

Cover design by Laura Duffy
Book design by Amit Dey

Printed in the United States of America

CONTENTS

———— ♦ ♦ ♦ ————

PREFACE

◆ ◆ ◆

Do you remember your first camera? Was it one that you had to pop open to insert a roll of film? If you are a baby boomer, you may recall such an apparatus; however, if you are a millennial or of generation Z, you might be wondering what I am talking about.

Long before cell phones, we happily and proudly used hand-held cameras. It was a luxury item! The hand-held camera was our only means of taking photographs. Who would ever think that one day your telephone would also take pictures?

During the days of my youth, we had phones that were mounted on the walls. We had telephones that were stationary on the desk. And we had what was known as party lines. Often without our awareness, the party lines gave individuals access to one another's conversations. Too often, people could listen in on your conversation without any notification. I would imagine it would be a good practice not to talk about someone because they could be listening in to your conversation.

At the age of 14, I remember purchasing my first camera. My, how exciting that was! I always loved pictures, drawings, and photography, and would do just about anything to have a camera and a fresh roll of film. There was something about a new roll of film that enhanced my excitement.

Back in the 70's, many photographs were printed in black and white, and color photos were becoming more popular. Needless to say, the printing of the black and white picture was proportionally less expensive than the printing of the color film. While living in the country, one of the best ways for me to get my photos printed was to put them in the mail. The other option was to have them printed in the local drug store but that was very expensive. I would mail my pictures off for printing, and a bonus was getting two pictures printed for the price of one. What an incentive! Needless to say, to me, that was the best deal ever. Taking and printing pictures was cyclical. It was a customary cycle for me. I would order my film in the mail and after taking a roll of pictures, I would send them off to be printed. With tip-toe anticipation, I awaited their arrival in the country mail.

During the weeks while I was waiting for the pictures to arrive, I would go shopping at the local dime store for the best photo album in town. Perhaps some of you remember Rose's or Woolworth's department stores. Rose's is where I would shop to find a photo album with transparent cover pages. When I could not find the sticky pages with the transparent cover pages, I would purchase the album that required tabs for holding pictures in place. The self-placed tabs indicated the space where the photograph was to be inserted. Regardless of the album style or filming timing, I was excited about the pictorial journey, and I pray you will find your thirst for reflection on the photos and illustrations in my book, *Soul Care in African American Practice*, to be transformative and empowering.

You have heard it said, "a picture is worth a thousand words." And I totally agree. Pictures often speak in the depth of places that our mere vocabulary cannot articulate. Pictures speak to individuals based upon their life experiences. Pictures speak and reveal truths that would otherwise go unnoticed. Yes! A picture is worth inexpressible measures, even beyond a thousand words.

During our time together in this workbook, we will not only look at a few pictures. Together, we will travel through time and behold the glory of the Lord through sacred lenses. Such a discipline is identified as *Visio Divina*. *Visio Divina* is a Latin word that means "divine seeing." What a blessing to have the gifted opportunity to desirously search for revelation from a picture, a sketch, or an illustration. Let us journey together as we seek to see through the eyes of the Divine…through the eyes of God.

Visio Divina calls us to meditate in a slower fashion than normal as we invite God to speak to and through us from a depth that exceeds what normally would meet our visual senses. This type of learning embarks upon insights and revelation that may normally be disregarded. *Visio Divina* is a calling to journey with God to see from a heavenly perspective.

In 1972, I entered my freshman year at North Carolina Central University in Durham, North Carolina. It was here that I pursued my undergraduate major in Clothing and Textiles, with a minor in Fashion and Design. What a beautiful major and experience. I thoroughly enjoyed learning about the history of fashion, drawing designs on paper, sketching bodily figures, and developing unique patterns. Once sketches and designs were established, patterns and fabrics had to be chosen. Artwork and textiles were part of my daily journey. Little did I know that even then, God was visually preparing me to see deeper and further than what was on the mere paper.

Designing fashions requires creativity, insight, and desire. It was the combination of taking photographs and a God-gifted eye for clothing design that undergirded my passion for *Visio Divina*. *Visio Divina* requires the visual expectation to see what you ordinarily would miss with just a glance. Such a spiritual discipline is undergirded with prayer, as we seek to hear God speak to the very depths of our souls.

In addition to textiles, pictures, artwork, and photographs, *Visio Divina* is all around us in the form of God's splendid creation. Nature speaks from the heavens to the sky, to the mountains, to the trees, through the ocean, the grains of sand on the beach, the buds of flowers in the garden, and the blades of grass in the field. As you practice *Visio Divina*, I encourage you to pause and pay attention to the intricate light in the spaces of the world. Notice shadows and shapes that would normally go unnoticed. Focus on diversity of tones, color, and movement of lines. Every leaf is unique, and every fingerprint is divine.

The world around us is inundated with postures, poses, and holy landscaping that graciously waits for us to stop and literally smell the roses. With that I say, let us begin the journey of Soul Care while practicing the discipline of *Visio Divina*. Welcome to the world of sacred artistry. Welcome to the sacred space of God's divine revelation to us, as we seek to see through his eyes. His sacred creation!

Please note that *Visio Divina* can occur in a small group or it can be practiced alone. Diverse ages, ethnicities, and dimensions of spirituality can engage in this discipline.

Let us begin with prayer.

Most gracious God,

I am humbled by the universe and the creation you made for your purpose and for your glory. I am in awe of your majesty and the radiance of the colors in the world that were created for us creatures to behold. Thank you for painting the world with your holy brush and carving out humanity's coloration in your image.

Dear God, as I travel through this Visio Divina journey with you, help me to see clearly. Help me to see like I've never seen before and help me to see through your lenses. Just like you removed the scales from the apostle Paul's eyes (Acts 9:1-19), please remove any kind or form of scale from my eyes. This I pray, in Jesus' Name. Amen.

Let's get started.

Visio Guidelines

1. Make sure you are in a comfortable space where you can spend 30-60 minutes (preferably, but shorter time is good as well).

2. Ask God to speak to you through the discipline of noticing an item or picture.

3. Listen for his still, small voice.

4. Partake in some breathing exercises. Inhale and exhale a few times.

5. During *Visio Divina*, remember to embrace your first impression but also (simultaneously) hold it loosely because God has so much to share with you.

6. Sit with the portion of the first visual intake and focus on what you saw. Give this your undivided attention.

7. Allow your mind to absorb detail(s) that you may have previously overlooked.

8. Pay attention to coloring, shading, shadows, lines, and the like.

9. Resist the temptation to wander off at other portions of scenery. Focus on a particular area.

10. Journal about your experience.

11. Sit with this time and absorb, notice and bathe in the comfort of *Visio Divina*.

12. Seal this sacred time in prayer.

In addition to practicing *Visio Divina* in this workbook, you will also have the opportunity to practice the discipline of *Lectio Divina*. Both *Visio Divina* and *Lectio Divina* are Latin terms. *Lectio Divina* means "sacred reading." When you practice *Lectio Divina*, you give a sacred passage your undivided attention. The process of spiritual absorption and reflection is the same as in *Visio Divina*. In *Visio Divina*, your focus is on a work of art and in *Lectio Divina*, your focus is on a phrase or word. Please see the definition for *Lectio Divina* and four main steps found in *Soul Care in African American Practice* on pages 35-36.

Soul Care Workbook Guidelines:

In this Soul Care Workbook, you will be given the opportunity to reflect on the cover of the book and the cover of the workbook. In this journal, you now have more space to write your response to the questions at the end of the chapters. Please note that the wording in some cases may differ slightly and that there are some additional questions.

In addition to your journaling reflection, in each chapter, I have included a scripture that you can use when practicing the discipline of *Lectio Divina*. I also encourage you to memorize the scripture and to consider it as a foundational passage for writing your personal prayer.

We will begin our time of *Visio Divina* by turning our undivided attention to the cover of the companion book, *Soul Care in African American Practice*.

1. Spend some time practicing the discipline of noticing. This discipline calls you to pause, stop, and see with fresh eyes. As you hone in on the cover of the book, what do you notice?

2. Where do you see yourself in or on the cover design?

_____

_____

_____

_____

_____

_____

3. Allow the cover to minister to you. How does it speak to you personally?

_____

_____

_____

_____

_____

_____

_____

_____

4. How could the cover design of the book possibly or prophetically speak to our nation?

_____

_____

_____

_____

_____

_____

_____

_____

Now, let's answer similar questions for the cover of this workbook.

As you reflect on the points above, look at the cover of the Soul Care Workbook.

1. What do you notice? What in the drawing speaks to you?

_____

_____

_____

_____

_____

2. Where do you see yourself in the cover design? How and why?

_____

_____

_____

_____

_____

3. How does the cover of the workbook speak to you personally?

_____

_____

_____

_____

_____

4. How could the workbook cover design possibly speak to our nation and its leadership?

_____

_____

_____

_____

5. Write a prayer based upon the cover(s) *Visio Divina* reflections and comments.

_____

_____

_____

_____

_____

_____

Questions

So often we just quickly move into the exercise of answering a question or questions without pausing to think of the thought that goes behind the question(s) and its projected or expected outcome.

Questions are designed to cause us to think deeper and consequently encounter moments of personal, group, or corporate transformation. Questions are growth tools that seek to draw the utmost truth out of our souls and minds. The questions throughout the book and journal, *Soul Care in African American Practice*, are reflective and thoughtful, based upon each of the ten chapters on African American spiritual leaders who practiced or who are currently practicing spiritual disciplines. In each chapter, I have identified a spiritual leader and correlated a discipline with their spiritual journey. I have also included questions in the introduction and the conclusion of the book.

Let us now turn our attention to the questions at the introduction of the book.

INTRODUCTION

— ♦ ♦ ♦ —

QUESTIONS FOR REFLECTION

1. Why is it important to look at prayer, spiritual direction, and soul care from an African American perspective?

2. Locate the Middle Passage map. Take a few minutes to allow the waters and the routes to speak to you. What are you hearing and sensing?

3. Now pay close attention to the image of African slaves on page 14. Notice how crowded they were. Take a few minutes to reflect on the faces, bodies, and chains. What speaks to you?

_____

_____

_____

_____

_____

_____

4. Together we seek to grasp a better understanding of spiritual direction and soul care from an African American perspective. Being mindful of the images you just reflected on and the reading you just encountered, what are your thoughts about spiritual direction and soul care from an African American perspective?

_____

_____

_____

_____

_____

_____

5. How was the Middle Passage a dark night of the soul?

_____

_____

_____

_____

_____

_____

6. As indicated in this chapter, persons of African descent were committed to the discipline of faith. Faith sustained them and empowered them with hope. In what area(s) of your life have you found yourself having to press into a greater dimension of the faith that abides in you?

_____

_____

_____

_____

_____

_____

7. During slavery, it was impermissible for persons of color to worship freely. Recently, I visited the Museum of the Bible in Washington, D.C. where I saw a copy of the slave Bible—a Bible written for slaves to keep them in bondage by extracting words of freedom. What are your thoughts about this Bible? See page 24.

_____

_____

_____

_____

_____

8. How do you think slavery has affected the way the church looks today?

_____

_____

_____

_____

_____

9. How has your spiritual history affected how and where you choose to worship?

_____

_____

_____

_____

_____

_____

10. Why do you think most places of worship have predominately one ethnicity? Is this a healthy community? If so, how so? If not, why not?

_____

_____

_____

_____

_____

_____

11. Would you consider changing your place of worship? Why or why not?

_____

_____

_____

_____

_____

_____

12. Take the time to discuss your perspective on some of these questions with someone that does not look like you. If you need more space, please journal in the extra space at the back of the workbook.

_____
_____
_____
_____
_____

Inhumane Circumstances

1. On page 14 of *Soul Care in African American Practice*, you will find a picture of Africana slaves stacked on a ship. What thoughts are unveiling in your mind? What pain are you feeling or lack thereof? Please share them in the space below. You will find more space for writing in the back of this journal.

_____
_____
_____
_____
_____

2. Our society continues to brutally treat persons. What are some ways you sense African Americans are mistreated today?

_____
_____
_____
_____
_____

3. What are some ways our society can overcome such behavior?

_____

_____

_____

_____

_____

_____

Even though the photo on page 14 reflects men of color, suffering for the Africana woman is also inevitable. Here is a challenging and painfilled truth:

Women were beaten when they refused to sexually succumb to their slave-master. "Dis ol' man now, would start beatin' her nekkid till the blood run down her back to her heels. I took an 'seed th' whelps an 'scars for my own self wid dese her two eyes."[1]

1. Please share your reflections on this quote.

_____

_____

_____

_____

_____

_____

_____

_____

---

[1] Goatley, David Emmanuel, *Were you there? Godforsakenness in Slave Religion.* New York: Orbis Books, 1996, 25.

Scripture for *Lectio Divina*

> **Galatians 5:1** - *It is for freedom that Christ has set us free. Stand firm, then, and do not let yourselves be burdened again by a yoke of slavery.* (NIV)

Spend some time memorizing this scripture. This scripture was transformative for me and I pray it is the same for you.

As you focus on the introduction and the verse above, write a prayer that ministers to your soul through this passage.

_____

_____

_____

_____

_____

_____

_____

—— ♦♦♦ ——

PART ONE

SPIRITUAL DIRECTION

and

SPIRITUAL DISCIPLINES

—— ♦♦♦ ——

1

DR. FREDERICK DOUGLASS

Born: February 1818 - Cordova, Maryland
Died: February 20, 1895 - Washington, D.C.

Spiritual Direction and Lectio Divina

— ◆ ◆ ◆ —

QUESTIONS FOR REFLECTION

1. When you look at the illustration of Jesus as the Good Shepherd on page 9, who and what do you see? What are you spiritually sensing?

2. Can you see yourself embracing the art of stillness while you meditate on the illustration on page 9? Why or why not?

3. In what area(s) of your life do you sense God calling you to be still?

4. Are there any particular times you sense God is calling you to be still in his presence?

5. How is God calling you?

6. Why is God calling you?

_____

_____

_____

_____

_____

_____

_____

Scripture for Spiritual Direction and *Lectio Divina*

Joshua 1:8 - *Keep this Book of the Law always on your lips; meditate on it day and night, so that you may be careful to do everything written in it. Then you will be prosperous and successful.* (NIV)

Spend some time memorizing this scripture. I have found this passage to be true in my life. Meditation is one of my favorite disciplines.

As you focus on this chapter and the verse above, write a prayer that ministers to your soul through this chapter and this passage.

_____

_____

_____

_____

_____

_____

_____

2

REV. DR. MARTIN LUTHER KING, JR.

Born: January 15, 1929 - Atlanta, Georgia
Assassinated: April 4, 1968 - Memphis, Tennessee

Spiritual Direction and Prayer

—————— ♦ ♦ ♦ ——————

QUESTIONS FOR REFLECTION

1. Prayerfully and slowly, read the following:

In this manner, therefore, pray:

Our Father in heaven, Hallowed be Your name.
Your kingdom come. Your will be done on earth as it is in heaven.
Give us this day our daily bread.
And forgive us our debts, as we forgive our debtors.
And do not lead us into temptation but deliver us from the evil one.
For Yours is the kingdom and the power and the glory forever.

Amen.

For if you forgive men their trespasses, your heavenly Father will
also forgive you. But if you do not forgive men their trespasses,
neither will your Father forgive your trespasses.
Moreover, when you fast, do not be like the hypocrites, with a sad countenance.
For they disfigure their faces that they may appear to men to be fasting. Assuredly, I say to
you, they have their reward (Matthew 6:9-16 NKJV).

2. What words stand out in this prayer?

_____

_____

_____

_____

_____

_____

3. Read the prayer a second time, even slower. Choose a phrase or a word that ministers to you. How does it speak to you?

_____

_____

_____

_____

_____

_____

4. Take a minute to pause and reflect on what Jesus is saying to his disciples. How does this prayer speak to disciples today that is different or the same from 2,000 years ago?

_____

_____

_____

_____

_____

_____

5. How does this overall prayer speak to you as a call to action?

_____

_____

_____

_____

_____

_____

_____

6. Being mindful that Dr. King was the son of a preacher, I am confident he knew this prayer. How do you think this prayer spoke to him?

_____

_____

_____

_____

_____

_____

_____

7. Considering the context of his involvement in justice and civil rights, how would it speak to him differently than it speaks to you?

_____

_____

_____

_____

_____

_____

_____

8. Define justice in your own words.

_____

_____

_____

_____

_____

_____

_____

9. How can you be a conduit that God uses to implement justice?

_____

_____

_____

_____

_____

_____

10. How does the prayer that Jesus taught his disciples connect to the acronym of the ACTS prayer? Please see pages 48-49 in the book.

_____

_____

_____

_____

_____

_____

11. Identify and specify where you see examples of adoration, confession, thanksgiving, and supplication?

_____

_____

_____

_____

_____

_____

_____

Scripture for Spiritual Direction and Prayer

> **Matthew 6:9** - *Our Father in heaven, Hallowed be Your name.* (NIV)

Spend some time memorizing this scripture. There is nothing more beautiful than meditation on the sovereignty of Almighty God!

As you focus on this chapter and the verse above, write a prayer that ministers to your soul through this chapter and this passage.

_____

_____

_____

_____

_____

_____

Share your prayer with someone you love.

3

DR. ROSA PARKS

(Received more than 43 Honorary Doctorate Degrees)
Born: February 4, 1913 - Tuskegee, Alabama
Died: October 24, 2005 - Detroit, Michigan

Meditation and Contemplation

———————— ♦ ♦ ♦ ————————

QUESTIONS FOR REFLECTION

1. Identify ways you see Dr. Parks as a person of meditation.

_____

_____

_____

_____

_____

2. Identify ways you see Dr. Parks as a person of contemplation.

_____

_____

_____

_____

_____

3. Is there a family member, friend, or colleague that you can identify as a person of meditation and/or contemplation?

_____

_____

_____

_____

_____

_____

_____

4. How is that person's practice of these disciplines similar to Dr. Parks's? Why is that important?

_____

_____

_____

_____

_____

_____

_____

5. How is that person's practice of these disciplines different from Dr. Parks's? Why is that important?

_____

_____

_____

_____

_____

_____

6. Imagine sitting on the bus like Dr. Parks. Put yourself in her shoes. What thoughts do you find circulating in your mind?

_____

_____

_____

_____

_____

_____

_____

7. What are some of your experiences of meditation?

_____

_____

_____

_____

_____

_____

_____

_____

8. What are some of your experiences of contemplation?

_____

_____

_____

_____

_____

_____

_____

9. How is God calling you deeper into meditation and contemplation?

_____

_____

_____

_____

_____

_____

_____

Scripture for Meditation and Contemplation

> **Joshua 1:8** - *Keep this Book of the Law always on your lips; meditate on it day and night, so that you may be careful to do everything written in it. Then you will be prosperous and successful.* (NIV)

Spend some time memorizing this scripture. There is nothing more beautiful than meditation on the sovereignty of Almighty God!

As you focus on this chapter and the verse above, write a prayer that ministers to your soul through this chapter and this passage.

_____

_____

_____

_____

_____

_____

_____

_____

4

DR. DARRELL GRIFFIN

Born: May 2, 1965 - Kenosha, Wisconsin

Spiritual Direction and Soul Care

——————————— ♦ ♦ ♦ ———————————

QUESTIONS FOR REFLECTION

1. Reflect on the congregation(s) you are aware of that are receptive to the practice of spiritual direction and soul care. Please identify and name them (if any).

2. Why do you think there are so few (or none), if that is your response?

3. How can the language of spiritual direction and soul care, along with other spiritual disciplines, be more easily accepted into faith communities?

_____

_____

_____

_____

_____

_____

_____

4. Do you have a spiritual director or someone that provides soul care for you? Why or why not?

_____

_____

_____

_____

_____

_____

_____

5. If you have a spiritual director or soul care giver, thank God for him or her. If you do not have someone to tend to your soul, take this time with God to reveal one to you. I am praying the prayer of agreement with you. In Jesus' name. Amen.

_____

_____

_____

_____

_____

6. As you reflect on Dr. Griffin's journey (pages 64-76) as a pastor, do you see any similarities between him and your pastor? Perhaps you see qualities that you would like reinforced in your church. If so, what are they?

_____

_____

_____

_____

_____

_____

Scripture for Spiritual Direction and Soul Care

> **John 14:26** - *But the Advocate, the Holy Spirit, whom the Father will send in my name, will teach you all things and will remind you of everything I have said to you.* (NIV)

Spend some time memorizing this scripture. Think about how God is the ultimate Spiritual Director and the impact of his direction in your life.

God gave me this scripture when I needed his divine direction in my life. At one time, I thought I was losing my mind, but this passage kept me and reminded me of how his mind is in mine.

As you focus on this chapter and the verse above, write a prayer that ministers to your soul through this chapter and this passage.

_____

_____

_____

_____

_____

5

DR. RENITA WEEMS

Born: June 26, 1954 - Atlanta, Georgia

Detachment and Attachment in Spiritual Direction

———————— ♦ ♦ ♦ ————————

QUESTIONS FOR REFLECTION

1. In what areas do you identify with Dr. Weems? Please reference pages 77-89 in the book.

_____

_____

_____

_____

_____

2. How is your life different from hers?

_____

_____

_____

_____

_____

_____

3. Finding quality time to spend with God requires pulling away from people and activities. What are some of the things God is calling you to pull away from? Please take a few minutes (or as long as you need) before writing out your reflection on this question.

4. What do you see as some of the main reasons people do not have time to spend with God?

5. What changes will you have to incorporate to continue to carve out sacred time with God?

Scripture for Detachment and Attachment in Spiritual Direction

> **John 10:10** - *The thief comes only to steal and kill and destroy; I have come that they may have life, and have it to the full.* (NIV)

Spend some time memorizing this scripture.

As you focus on detaching from the cares of this world and attaching more to Yahweh, think about the verse above and write a precious prayer that ministers to your soul through this chapter and this passage.

_____

_____

_____

_____

_____

_____

Before we dive into the second section of the book, let us once again reflect on the cover of the book and the cover of the workbook. What similarities do you see and what is different about the two covers?

_____

_____

_____

_____

_____

_____

_____

PART TWO

◆◆◆

PRAYER DISCIPLINES

◆◆◆

6

DR. HAROLD CARTER

Born: 1937 - Selma, Alabama
Died: May 30, 2013 - Baltimore, MD

Prayer and Generational Spiritual Foundation

———————— ◆ ◆ ◆ ————————

QUESTIONS FOR REFLECTION

1. Do you practice the discipline of prayer in your personal life? When did it begin and what circumstances were instrumental in its development?

_____

_____

_____

_____

_____

2. What does the discipline of prayer look like? Do you have a private space or prayer closet that draws you to be with your Lord?

_____

_____

_____

_____

_____

3. Do you want to make any changes in your personal prayer life and what are they?

_____

_____

_____

_____

_____

_____

4. If you do not desire to make any prayer changes, please share why you do not.

_____

_____

_____

_____

_____

_____

5. Is prayer a tradition in your family and where and when did you see the practice? If not, please skip to number 6.

_____

_____

_____

_____

_____

_____

6. You have indicated that prayer is not an ongoing discipline in your family. How do you sense God drawing you to make it part of your tradition?

_____

_____

_____

_____

_____

_____

7. Please pray and ask God to give you an entry point. He sincerely desires that you spend time in prayer.

_____

_____

_____

_____

_____

_____

8. If prayer is currently taking place in your family, what changes do you desire to make?

_____

_____

_____

_____

_____

_____

9. What does the prayer life environment in your church look like?

_____

_____

_____

_____

_____

_____

_____

10. How would you like to see prayer differently in your church?

_____

_____

_____

_____

_____

_____

_____

11. Ask God to give you the influence to make transformative prayer more central in the life of your church. Write a prayer to that effect.

_____

_____

_____

_____

_____

_____

_____

12. On page 97, several persons are identified as prayer leaders. Please identify someone you know as a prayer leader and how their impact affects the faith community?

_____

_____

_____

_____

_____

_____

_____

Scripture for Prayer and Generational Spiritual Foundation

James 5:16 - *Therefore confess your sins to each other and pray for each other so that you may be healed. The prayer of a righteous person is powerful and effective.* (NIV)

Spend some time memorizing this confession scripture.

As you focus on this chapter and the verse above, write a prayer that ministers to your soul through this chapter and this passage.

Is there anything on your heart that you need to confess for your prayers to be more effective? Please share below or write a prayer.

_____

_____

_____

_____

_____

_____

_____

7

DR. JESSICA INGRAM

Born: July 25, 1947 – Little Rock, Arkansas

Prayer and Spiritual Direction

———————— ◆ ◆ ◆ ————————

QUESTIONS FOR REFLECTION

1. What is the correlation between prayer and spiritual direction?

————————————————————————
————————————————————————
————————————————————————
————————————————————————
————————————————————————
————————————————————————

2. As we continue to look at the relationship between prayer and spiritual direction, which would you say is more important as it relates to the spiritual disciplines?

————————————————————————
————————————————————————
————————————————————————
————————————————————————
————————————————————————
————————————————————————

3. If you have a spiritual director or someone who tends to your soul, how would you describe that person's prayer life?

4. From your perspective, during a spiritual direction session, what percentage of the time should be spent in prayer?

5. Being mindful that there are listening as well as speaking prayers, in what ways can a spiritual director balance the two in a direction session?

6. How do you incorporate both listening and speaking into your prayer time?

_____

_____

_____

_____

_____

7. Dr. Ingram is a woman of influence. What in the chapter (pages 105-111) about her
    grasps your attention?

_____

_____

_____

_____

_____

Scripture for Prayer and Spiritual Direction

> **I Thessalonians 5:16-18** - *Rejoice always, pray continually, give thanks in all
> circumstances; for this is God's will for you in Christ Jesus.* (NIV)

Spend some time memorizing this scripture.

As you focus on this chapter and the verse above, write a prayer that ministers to your soul
through this chapter and this passage. Even though these verses are short and to the point,
they are power-packed with insight and direction. What an awesome encouragement to
you to pray without ceasing (KJV) and to pray continuously (NIV).

_____

_____

_____

8

DR. CORETTA SCOTT KING

(More than 60 Honorary Doctorates)
Born: April 27, 1927 - Marion, Alabama
Died: January 30, 2006 - Rosarito Beach, Mexico

Prayer and Civil Rights

——————— ♦ ♦ ♦ ———————

QUESTIONS FOR REFLECTION

1. Imagine yourself wearing Dr. Coretta Scott King's shoes. Her husband is away serving. Her children need her. One community looks up to her as a "shero," while another community may see her as the enemy. As you reflect on walking in her shoes for a day, what would you imagine her prayer life to look like?

2. Describe what you see and hear as it relates to Dr. Coretta Scott King's spiritual journey.

_____

_____

_____

_____

_____

_____

3. How do you think prayer influenced her husband, Rev. Dr. King Martin Luther King, Jr., and the civil rights movement?

_____

_____

_____

_____

_____

_____

4. Write out a prayer for the King family. Consider mailing it to them. A good start for sending it would be Ebenezer Baptist Church, 101 Jackson St. NE, Atlanta, GA 30312. However, you may pursue a more thorough search as you are led.

_____

_____

_____

_____

_____

_____

5. Write a prayer for members of Emanuel Church in Charleston, South Carolina. Consider mailing it to the church at Mother Emanuel AME Church, 110 Calhoun St, Charleston, SC 29401.

_____

_____

_____

_____

_____

_____

_____

Scripture for Prayer and Civil Rights

> **I Timothy 6:12** - *Fight the good fight of the faith. Take hold of the eternal life to which you were called when you made your good confession in the presence of many witnesses.* (NIV)

Spend some time memorizing this scripture.

As you focus on this chapter and the verse above, write a prayer that ministers to your soul and the content of this chapter. You may also write any additional reflection in the space below.

_____

_____

_____

_____

_____

_____

_____

_____

9

DR. JAMES WASHINGTON

Born: April 24, 1948 - Knoxville, Tennessee
Died: May 3, 1997 - New York, New York

Prayer and Rest

———————— ♦ ♦ ♦ ————————

QUESTIONS FOR REFLECTION

1. What are some disciplines you can incorporate into your life that can be guiding tools as you experience restful prayer?

_____

_____

_____

_____

_____

2. Do you have a difficult time pulling away from a busy schedule? Why or why not?

_____

_____

_____

_____

_____

3. How often do you go away on vacation?

4. When is your sabbath, and what does it look like?

5. What is God calling you to accomplish that you know cannot be carried out without your obedience to practicing the sabbath?

6. In what ways does our society encourage busyness?

_____

_____

_____

_____

_____

_____

_____

_____

7. How does our society reinforce rest?

_____

_____

_____

_____

_____

_____

_____

8. Who do you know whose love language is rest? How do you see it demonstrated in that person's life?

_____

_____

_____

_____

_____

_____

_____

9. What do you need to do differently to incorporate more relaxation into your schedule?

_____

_____

_____

_____

_____

_____

_____

10. When and under what circumstances do you foresee rest becoming a lifestyle for you?

_____

_____

_____

_____

_____

_____

11. List at least five people who you can prayerfully and gingerly encourage to come away from the busyness of society and invite them to focus on just being.

_____

_____

_____

_____

_____

_____

Scripture for Prayer and Rest

> **Psalm 23:2-3** - *He makes me lie down in green pastures, he leads me beside quiet waters, he refreshes my soul. He guides me along the right paths for his name's sake.* (NIV)

Spend some time memorizing this scripture.

As you focus on this chapter and the verse above, write a prayer that ministers to your soul through this chapter and this passage. I encourage you to honor God by receiving the gift of rest.

_____

_____

_____

_____

_____

_____

_____

_____

10

DR. HOWARD THURMAN

Born: November 18, 1899 - Daytona Beach, Florida
Died: April 10, 1981 - San Francisco, California

Prayer and Suffering

———————— ◆ ◆ ◆ ————————

QUESTIONS FOR REFLECTION

1. Think about a cause you are willing to sacrifice for, or a mission you are willing to suffer for because of your conviction about that particular situation. What area(s) of focus comes to mind?

_____

_____

_____

_____

_____

2. Why is this cause so important to you? What happened in your life for you to be willing to suffer for this concern?

_____

_____

_____

_____

3. Can you think of a time when you should have stood up for a cause?

_____

_____

_____

_____

_____

_____

_____

4. When did you consider paying the price but decided not to stand for justice as it related to that particular matter?

_____

_____

_____

_____

_____

_____

_____

5. What thoughts went on in your mind that hindered you from taking a sacrificial stance?

_____

_____

_____

_____

_____

_____

_____

6. What comes to mind as you reflect on the signs of the time, the condition of the world we live in, and the various causes people suffer for?

_____

_____

_____

_____

_____

_____

_____

_____

_____

7. List a situation(s) where you have seen others suffer to make a difference.

_____

_____

_____

_____

_____

_____

_____

_____

_____

Scripture for Prayer and Suffering

I Peter 2:21 – _To this you were called, because Christ suffered for you, leaving you an example, that you should follow in his steps._ (NIV)

Spend some time memorizing this scripture.

As you focus on this chapter and the verse above, write a prayer that ministers to your soul through this chapter and this passage. Yes, it is challenging to embrace the discipline of suffering. However, suffering can draw us closer to fuller dependence on Yahweh as it produces spiritual character.

_____

_____

_____

_____

_____

_____

_____

_____

CONCLUSION

—— ♦ ♦ ♦ ——

REFLECTION

1. How do you think God sees color, ethnicity, or race?

_____

_____

_____

_____

_____

_____

_____

_____

2. Identify a time on your spiritual journey when you encountered an epiphany related to racial diversity or the lack thereof?

_____

_____

_____

_____

_____

_____

_____

_____

3. "Reflecting on the existence and consequences of the blatant racial divide saddens numerous hearts." What are your thoughts about this statement?

_____

_____

_____

_____

_____

_____

_____

4. How can we all become more aware of the Spirit of God who does not show any partiality?

_____

_____

_____

_____

_____

_____

_____

5. God sees us scurrying from one task to another and from one location to another. If he spoke audibly to us about such behavior, what do you think he would say?

_____

_____

_____

_____

_____

_____

6. How does busyness affect the soul?

7. What does spiritual formation look like in your current faith community?

8. What progress in equality do you think has made the most impact in the African American faith community?

9. Resurrection suggests that something that was dead or dormant has come to life. What in your personal life needs to be resurrected?

_____

_____

_____

_____

_____

_____

_____

10. How has the plight of the African American church affected the shape of Christendom?

_____

_____

_____

_____

_____

_____

11. What spiritual disciplines have shaped your spiritual journey?

_____

_____

_____

_____

_____

_____

12. What are some things that keep you too busy to spend time with God?

13. Decide today to come away from the busyness of life and develop some new habits. What new habits might you start?

14. Why is it important for people of African descent to be mindful of the spirituality of those who went before them?

15. How do prayer and spiritual direction nurture the soul of an individual?

_____

_____

_____

_____

_____

_____

16. What are some of the challenges to keeping your commitment to spend more time with the Lord?

_____

_____

_____

_____

_____

_____

17. What is your prayer for your spiritual legacy? In other words, what do you want to be remembered for spiritually?

_____

_____

_____

_____

_____

_____

18. From your experience, in what ways is the spirituality of the African American tradition different from that of other cultures?

_____

_____

_____

_____

_____

_____

_____

19. As we move forward in the twenty-first century, how can the African American faith community and church seek to implement the disciplines of spiritual direction and soul care?

_____

_____

_____

_____

_____

_____

_____

20. How are you sensing God is calling you to be more attentive to souls around you?

_____

_____

_____

_____

_____

_____

21. In what ways have African desert fathers impacted the twenty-first-century church?

_____

_____

_____

_____

_____

_____

Scripture for Conclusion

> **Philippians 1:6** - ...*being confident of this, that he who began a good work in you will carry it on to completion until the day of Christ Jesus.* (NIV)

Spend some time memorizing this scripture.

As you focus on this last chapter and the verse above, write a prayer that ministers to your soul. What an assurance to know that God always completes the work he begins in us!

_____

_____

_____

_____

_____

_____

_____

_____

_____

_____

The above sections reflect on the ten spiritual leaders mentioned in the book *Soul Care in African American Practice*. I trust you have enjoyed your time in prayer and reflection with them.

It is at this juncture in the workbook that we turn our attention to four persons that passed in 2020. I am cognizant that numerous others passed. However, these are the four I have chosen to highlight under the theme of Black Lives Matter Soul Care. In the section below, we are not necessarily looking for the practice of spiritual discipline in the lives of Breonna Taylor, Ahmaud Arbery, George Floyd, or Robert Lewis. In this section, we are pausing to honor their lives and their contributions to society.

BLACK LIVES MATTER SOUL CARE

◆ ◆ ◆

Amidst the climate in our country, it is imperative that we pause to take a moment to reflect on the Black Lives Matter Movement. To much dismay, way too many lives of the past and present have been snuffed out prematurely and unjustly. In this section, we will take a sacred pause to intentionally reflect on lives that have gone on in 2020. It is during these times that we must have a greater commitment to care for our very souls. This is personal and corporate soul caring.

Chains of bondage and the spirit of oppression have been an intricate part of our African American history. Chains and ropes and guns and strangling have been part of our journey. Too often people of color die unjustly. Such was the case of George Floyd. On May 25, 2020, Mr. Floyd was strangled and suffocated. In agony and fear, he cried out "I can't breathe." Even though we are no longer in chains on a ship, we remain in chains behind bars and knees, oppression and suppression, injustices and discrimination.

1. Once again, take the time to reflect on the picture on page 14 in the book. What do you think are the thoughts of the enslaved chained persons?

_____

_____

_____

_____

_____

_____

_____

2. Imagine what they are thinking. How do they foresee their future, if at all?

_____

_____

_____

_____

_____

3. How is your life similar to and different from theirs?

_____

_____

_____

_____

_____

_____

4. Please write a prayer as you reflect on this photo on page 14.

_____

_____

_____

_____

_____

_____

The year 2020 was quite a year. At times it has been emotionally exhausting—that is exactly what I would like to say. Too many premature deaths. Consequently, our streets have been filled with protests due to the killings of men and women who died at the hand of those who are supposed to be protecting them. It is now that we pause to honor the life of Ahmaud Arbery, Breonna Taylor, and George Floyd.

BREONNA TAYLOR

Born: June 5, 1993 - Grand Rapids, Michigan
Died: March 13, 2020 - Louisville, Kentucky
Emergency Medical Technician

Please write a prayer as we pause to honor the life of Ms. Taylor.

_____

_____

_____

_____

_____

AHMAUD ARBERY

Born: May 8, 1994 - Brunswick, Georgia
Died: February 23, 2020 - Brunswick, Georgia
Former High School Linebacker

Ahmaud Arbery was jogging in his neighborhood outside Brunswick, Georgia on February 23, 2020. He was killed in a shooting after being chased by Gregory and Travis McMichael, a father and son.

Please write a prayer as you reflect on the life of Ahmaud Arbery.

_____

_____

_____

_____

_____

GEORGE FLOYD

Born: October 14, 1973 - Fayetteville, North Carolina
Died: May 25, 2020 - Minneapolis, Minnesota
Played Basketball and Football at Yates High School
Security Support for Salvation Army and Congo Latin Bistro

Officer Derek Chauvin knelt on Floyd's neck for eight minutes and 46 seconds. Mr. Floyd was handcuffed and lying face down and was continuously begging for his life by saying "I can't breathe." As a result of Mr. Floyd's death, protests were triggered around the world.

Please write a prayer in honor of George Floyd.

_____

_____

_____

_____

Black Lives Matter Contemplation, *Lectio Divina, Visio Divina*

On May 25, 2020, for eight minutes and 46 seconds, I would imagine (former police officer) Derek Chauvin's thoughts went something like this. I can't prove it, neither can you. But if I had to put words to his thoughts, I would imagine he thought something like this: "Oh what comfort and pleasure I have as I partake in holding him captive. His name does not matter. All that matters is I am in control. I got this. As a matter of fact, I can just relax in this moment and take pleasure in my power. Oh, how I waited for this encounter. I have paid dearly for this and I have the rights to restrain this person."

Any reflection?

_____

_____

_____

Let us now pause to honor the sacred life of a spiritual giant and civil solider.

JOHN ROBERT LEWIS

Born: February 21, 1940 - Troy, Alabama
Died: July 17, 2020 - Atlanta, Georgia
United States Representative and Civil Rights Leader

Mr. John Lewis was an advocate and leader for the Civil Rights Movement. A member of the Democratic Party, he was elected to Congress in 1986. We thank God for his transformative leadership and commitment to our country and the African American community.

Please write a noble prayer to honor this spiritual giant.

_____

_____

_____

_____

_____

_____

_____

_____

_____

_____

_____

_____

_____

_____

_____

_____

VISIO DIVINA AND COLORING

◆ ◆ ◆

Throughout this interactive workbook and the book, so much has been shared with you and others. Numerous pictures, sketches, and illustrations have been discussed. And now you can become the photographer, illustrator, or artist. In the space below, please post a picture, print, or draw your own masterpiece that depicts your current emotional state.

Perhaps you reflect on the last section of this book, the 2020 journey, or share a visual depicting your current state. Be creative. Pause and pray before coloring and prepare to discuss with others.

1. Once again, reflect on the pictures of the man and the lamb on pages 9 and 92 of *Soul Care in African American Practice*. What do you hear? What do you see?

_____

_____

_____

_____

_____

_____

_____

2. What do you notice now that is different from the first time you practiced *Visio Divina*?

_____

_____

_____

_____

_____

_____

_____

3. As you reflect on the definition of *Visio Divina*, look at the cover of the book. Please define *Visio Divina* in your own words.

_____

_____

_____

_____

_____

_____

_____

4. Where and how do you see yourself now in the cover design that is different from the beginning of you journaling?

_____

_____

_____

_____

_____

_____

5. How does the cover of the book speak to you personally?

_____

_____

_____

_____

_____

_____

6. How do you see the cover design speaking to our nation?

_____

_____

_____

_____

_____

_____

7. How do you see the cover design speaking to the church universal?

_____

_____

_____

_____

_____

_____

8. Where are you in the cover design? Do you see yourself? Why or why not?

_____

_____

_____

_____

_____

_____

Lectio Divina is a prayer method that typically immerses an individual in Scripture and helps them to hear God's voice through a particular passage and their reflection on it. *Lectio Divina* treats Scripture as the living, breathing Word of God. As praying people, we are called to slow down enough so that we can become aware of and attentive to God's holy presence. *Lectio Divina* can help us do just that as it prompts us to let the Word of God sink into us through repeated reading and contemplation of a passage.

Lectio Divina reminds us that God speaks in numerous prayer languages; sometimes with his mindful Word and some without such "spiritual" words. God speaks through emotions, tears, laughter, and sensations.

The sacred discipline of *Lectio Divina* has helped me to stop thinking of prayer as mostly talking and listening in their traditional forms and has enabled me to connect with

God much more comfortably and deeply, both biblically and through the evidence of life around me. The pause of *Lectio Divina* embraces the nature of God more holistically.

Let us now practice *Lectio Divina* by referring to the song "The Negro National Anthem" found on pages 152-153. Please read the lyrics and identify a verse or two that speaks to you. Ruminate on it and follow the steps of *Lectio Divina* found on pages 35-36 in the book.

1. What is God saying to you through this song?

_____

_____

_____

_____

_____

_____

2. Focus on three words. What directives are you hearing?

_____

_____

_____

_____

_____

_____

3. Now focus on one word that stands out the most? What are you hearing now?

_____

_____

_____

_____

_____

4. Please write a prayer as your response to God speaking to you.

_____

_____

_____

_____

_____

_____

_____

Below is a chart of the soul care spiritual leaders. Their date of birth, where they were born, their date of death, and where they were during their deaths. Below the chart, there is space to share how you see yourself connecting with them.

Name	Born	Location	Died	Location
Fredrick Douglass	2.1818	Cordova, MD	2.20.1895	Washington, D.C.
Martin Luther King, Jr.	1.15.1929	Atlanta, GA	4.4.1968	Memphis, TN
Rosa Parks	2.4.1913	Tuskegee, AL	10.24.2005	Detroit, MI
Darrell Griffin	5.2.1965	Kenosha, WI		
Renita Weems	6.26.1954	Atlanta, GA		
Harold Carter	1937	Selma, AL	5.30.2013	Baltimore, MD
Jessica Ingram	7.25.1947	Little Rock, AR		
Coretta Scott	4.27.1927	Marion, AL	1.30.2006	Rosarito Beach, Mexico
James Washington	4.24.1948	Knoxville, TN	5.3.1997	New York, NY
Howard Thurman	11.18.1899	Daytona Beach, FL	4.10.1981	San Francisco, CA

Name	Born	Location	Died	Location
Breonna Taylor	6.5.1993	Grand Rapids, MI	3.13.2020	Louisville, KY
Ahmaud Arbery	5.8.1994	Brunswick, GA	2.23.2020	Brunswick, GA
George Floyd	10.14.1973	Fayetteville, NC	5.25.2020	Minneapolis, MN
John Lewis	2.21.1940	Troy, AL	7.17.2020	Atlanta, GA
Barbara Peacock	2.22.1954	Whiteville, NC		
Your Name				

Use this space to share which spiritual leader you connect with and how.

_____

_____

_____

_____

_____

_____

_____

_____

_____

_____

_____

_____

_____

_____

_____

_____

Look Well To The Growing Edge

"All around us worlds are dying
and new worlds are being born;
all around us life is dying and life is being born.
The fruit ripens on the tree,
the roots are silently at work in the darkness of the earth against
a time when there shall be new lives,
fresh blossoms, green fruit.
Such is the growing edge!
It is the extra breath from the exhausted lung,
the one more thing to try when all else has failed, the upward reach of life
when weariness closes in upon all endeavor.
This is the basis of hope in moments of despair,
the incentive to carry on when times are out of joint and men
have lost their reason,
the source of confidence when worlds crash
and dreams whiten into ash.
The birth of a child —
Life's most dramatic answer to death — this is the growing
edge incarnate. Look well to the growing edge!" [2]

---

[2] Thurman, Howard, *Meditations of the Heart III: LIFE IS ALIVE*, #24, The Growing Edge, Friends United Press, Richmond, IN. 134.

NOTES

◆ ◆ ◆

Use the space below for additional reflections.

_____

_____

_____

_____

_____

_____

_____

_____

_____

_____

_____

_____

_____

_____

_____

_____

_____

_____

_____

_____

_____

_____

_____

_____

_____

_____

_____

_____

_____

_____

_____

_____

_____

_____

_____

_____

_____

Milton Keynes UK
Ingram Content Group UK Ltd.
UKHW021323160724
445750UK00044B/1515